@

MW01096412

A PREFERENCE FOR PREFERREDS:

ALL YOU NEED TO KNOW ABOUT INVESTING IN PREFERRED STOCK

by

Michael F. Greco, CFP®, ChFC

INTRODUCTION

I have been managing money for almost 20 years, and in that time I have found that financial advisors and investors alike understand surprisingly little about preferred stock. As a hybrid security between bonds and stock, so many people feel that it's not actually appropriate for them. Almost all of them couldn't be more wrong!

I have been using preferred stock in virtually all client portfolios throughout my career – even those whose objective is growth. Opportunities exist for investors to use preferred stock not just to produce income, but to produce relatively high levels of income – often higher than most investors realize. They help reduce volatility, hedge against market swings and can even help the growth oriented investor achieve their return expectations without as much risk as an all equity portfolio would require.

We have used preferred stock so often in client portfolios that one of them asked me if I could give them a fuller understanding of what these securities actually are, and why we've chosen to buy this one or that. I wrote this tome with the desire of creating a full, yet concise, primer on what any investor would need to know to understand these "off the beaten path" securities, so that they could feel more confident in determining if they're appropriate for them.

Inside I fully cover what preferred stock is, the different types of preferred stock, the risks and advantages of ownership and tax considerations. In the end, knowledge is power. This guide will give you the knowledge you need to help you navigate the markets and make money using preferred stock.

Table of Contents

Preferred Stock Issuance

Were one to look up a definition of preferred stock, the resulting text would likely state: "A class of ownership in a corporation that has a higher claim on the assets and earnings than common stock." While this is fully accurate, it is quite wanting and does nothing to express the complexity of this seemingly simple security. In order to fully understand what preferred stock (also known as preferred shares) actually is, one must understand how corporations raise capital.

Any corporation, whether it be public or private, requires capital. Even small sole proprietors (such as a one-man accounting firm, a hot dog vendor or window washing service) require some up-front capital in order to acquire the tools, goods and/or supplies needed to launch the enterprise. In the case of a small business, it is likely that an entrepreneur put up some of their own savings to provide the capital needed to commence operations. Larger businesses, even those that are classified as small business, may require additional capital for any number of reasons. Whatever the reason, as the reason is irrelevant to this explanation, there are only two basic means by which a corporation may raise capital – borrow or find investors.

Borrowing money is a strategy used by almost all large corporations. Borrowing may come in the form of bank loans, private placement debt (borrowing from a small, specific group of lenders) or bond issuance. In the end, no matter what avenue a corporation pursues to borrow money, the corporation has increased the amount of debt on their books. More accurately, the corporation has added liabilities to its balance sheet and increased their debt-to-equity ratio (assuming that the borrowed capital is not simply retained as cash). From an investor's perspective, the corporation's additional debt is a potential concern as the balance sheet has been eroded.

The other primary method of raising capital is to find investors. In order for an investor to place money into a corporation requires the issuance of stock. Note that we are not referencing an investor purchasing shares of a publicly traded company on an exchange, as that does nothing to increase cash on the balance sheet of the corporation. Finding investors requires that the company (or its current owners) put up for sale a portion of the business. Think of the television show *Shark Tank* where business owners sell a percentage of their firm to an investor for a capital infusion.

On a larger scale, particularly for public companies, corporations may issue a secondary offering. A secondary offering is where a corporation offers shares of the firm for sale from existing owners or treasury shares. An IPO (Initial Public Offering) is where a company "goes public" by offering shares for sale to the public via an exchange. A secondary offering is effectively the same process, although the company is already public and therefore it is not an <u>initial</u> offering.

Whether the issuance of stock is done by a massive S&P 500 publicly traded company, or a small corporation finding an outside investor to put capital into the firm, the result is always the same – dilution of existing shareholders. If a corporation increases its shares outstanding, existing shareholders have seen their stakes proportionately reduced by this issuance. (See illustration below.)

XYZ Corporation has 10 investors. Each of the existing shareholders owns an equal 10% stake in the firm. The firm needs funds to build a factory for expansion. In order to get the needed funding, the corporation sells a 30% stake to a group of interested investors.

Once the deal has been done, XYZ Corporation now has a number of additional investors, and each of the pre-issue shareholders have seen their ownership in the firm go from 10% to 7%.

For a relatively small company, the reduction in ownership stake may be a necessary, logical step in a strategic, long term plan. For larger, public companies, it is not the dilution of ownership stake that is upsetting, but the impact on share price. The share issuance is dilutive to investors in the same manner as above, but almost universally results in price depreciation corresponding to the proportionate increase in shares outstanding. Were a public company to increase its shares outstanding by 10%, there is a fairly equivalent reduction in price of the publicly traded shares. Under these circumstances, a stock trading at $40 may drop to $36 immediately following the announcement of the intention to issue the shares. The corresponding drop in price is upsetting to investors and a generally unattractive option to the majority of large, public companies.

Since debt issuance is detrimental to the balance sheet, and common stock offerings are unappealing to existing shareholders, enter the third option – Preferred Stock. Preferred stock is something of a hybrid security which carries characteristics of both debt and equity instruments. It is an attractive means to raise capital for many corporations as it is not common stock, so its issuance is not dilutive to existing shareholders. It is also not debt, so its issuance does not erode the balance sheet or carry as substantial of an effect on the corporation's credit rating. These two points makes issuance of preferred stock an attractive option to a corporation that is looking for long term capital.

ISSUANCE IN THE PRIVATE MARKET

In the public, secondary market one would not generally expect to find preferred stock with any special rights; however, private firms may offer preferred stock to new or existing investors with rights and provisions not afforded to holders of common stock. While preferred stock is generally a non-voting class of stock, private preferred shareholders may be granted special voting rights. In some instances, voting rights may be granted to preferred shareholders if dividends have not been paid for some predetermined length of time. Such shareholder provisions effectively may provide the investor(s) the ability to force payment on their claim should adequate corporate resources exist. In addition to special voting rights, preferred shareholders in private issuance may be conferred additional rights or

3

protections not commonly associated with public issues. Among them may be:

· Liquidation Preference in which holders are guaranteed to paid a fixed, or formulaic, amount prior to other shareholders in the event that the company is merged or sold.

· Anti-Dilution Protection provides that shareholders will be protected against dilution of their ownership interest should the corporation issue additional shares in the future. Most often this is seen in convertible securities where the conversion price will be adjusted downward to allow shareholders to retain their ownership percentage.

· The right to attend board of director meetings as an observer.

· Participation Rights which will provide the shareholder with any number of ways to participate in the growth of the company. Venture capitalists generally use participation rights as a means to demand voting seats on a board. These shares may also be structured such that holders receive the greater of their preferred dividend or dividends declared on common shares.

· The right to receive financial statements, or other company information on a regular basis.

· The right to meet with management at specified intervals or times.

· The right to inspect the corporation's properties and/or books and records.

· Preemptive rights on additional stock financings. While similar to anti-dilution protection, it allows the shareholder the opportunity to purchase future issued shares (be they common or preferred) prior to other parties.

· Rights of first refusal on the sale of founder stock. Again, similar to anti-dilution rights, but more robust as it potentially allows preferred shareholders the opportunity to gain control of the corporation via being first in line to acquire the stock.

· Co-sale rights on stock sales, which would permit the shareholder the opportunity to liquidate their holdings alongside other stock offerings.

· Drag Along rights, which allow majority shareholders to force minority shareholders to join in the sale of a company. In many instances, an acquirer will insist on becoming a 100% owner of the corporation, and a minority owner could thwart an acquisition by refusing to tender their shares. The Drag Along right would allow the majority shareholder the right to force the minority shareholder(s) to accept the same terms of sale that the majority shareholders receive.

Private corporations may find great flexibility in issuing various types of preferred stock when attempting to raise capital in anticipation of significant growth. In order to attract large outside investors, offering something more than a stated dividend may be necessary.

Dividends & The Capital Structure

We have noted the value to the corporation to issue preferred stock rather than debt or have a secondary offering, but what of the investor? Clearly, the investor must be motivated to acquire preferred stock rather than purchase the debt or equity of the issuing firm in order for the corporation to actually raise the capital. What is it about preferred stock that an investor finds appealing? The name "preferred" stock does not reference the corporation's preference to issue it or the investor's preference to buy it. The name references the security's place in the payment of dividends.

By definition, preferred shares are a class of stock and therefore equity. Preferred shares are no different than common shares in the nature of payments being considered dividends and not interest. (Interest is paid on debt.) Not all common stocks pay dividends, but all preferred shares do. Generally, preferred shares are non-voting, and if nothing else, the stated dividend is compensation to equity holders for not having a vote in the managerial decisions of the corporation. By law, dividends of preferred shares must be paid prior to dividends paid on common shares – hence the *preferred* nature of the dividend

As a general rule, preferred shares pay dividends on a quarterly basis. This is quite attractive to investors as bonds generally remit coupon payments semiannually. There are some preferred shares that remit dividends monthly as well. Payment frequency does not generally result in market price premium, but does allow investors to ladder income by selecting issues with varied payment dates.

Dividend payments function the same as for common stock. There are four important dates relating to payment of dividends:

· Declaration Date

This is the date that a corporation declares that a dividend is being paid. It may also be commonly referred to as the announcement date. It is generally considered a formality and not an important date when considering trading a dividend paying security.

· Record Date

When the dividend is declared by a corporation, the announcement will include the date of record. A shareholder of record is any investor who is listed on the books of the corporation as being a holder of the security. In order to fully grasp the concept of the record date, one must think back to a time when the books and records of a corporation where kept in a ledger. The company knew that you were an investor as your name was on the role of shareholders in their records. In the modern era, computers and brokerage firms have made this idea relatively obsolete, but the date remains a firm date to own a security in order to receive the dividend.

· Ex-Dividend Date

This is the date that the security will begin trading without ("ex") the dividend. The ex-dividend date is usually 2 business days prior to the record date. If an investor acquires the security prior to the ex-dividend date, he or she will receive the dividend when it is paid. Acquisition post ex-dividend date will provide the dividend to the previous owner of the security.

The market price of a security will generally fall by the amount of the dividend on the date it trades ex-dividend. For example, suppose XYZ Corporation pays a $0.25 dividend and is trading at $20 per share. On the ex-dividend date, the shares will trade at $19.75. It is quite intuitive why this occurs as purchasing the date prior will entitle the owner to a $0.25 payment, so why would someone acquire the security the following day for the same price and not be entitled to the $0.25 dividend?

· Payable Date

This is the date that the actual dividend is to be paid and received by shareholders.

It cannot be understated how crucial it is that preferred stock payments are dividends and not interest. As mentioned, unlike common stock, the dividends paid on preferred shares are not subject to discretionary revision by the corporation's board of directors. That is to say that the corporation may not change the dividend rate on a preferred share. For example, if a preferred issue is to pay $2 per year in dividends, the corporation may not elect to reduce it to $1.50 or raise it to $3 based on the company's performance. The dividend, if fixed, is a stated obligation.

It is not, however, a mandated obligation like repayment of debt. While the board may not discretionarily change the amount of the dividend, they may, in their discretion, elect to not make dividend payments. While we will discuss this risk in a later chapter, the simple fact is that a corporation may choose to not pay a dividend. They may choose to suspend the dividend for any period of time for whatever reason they choose. While the corporation is not permitted to remit common stock dividends should they have suspended preferred stock dividends, it is not a default as though they missed an interest payment on a bond or bank loan. It does not necessarily directly impact a company's credit rating, and so corporations would be more apt to take this step in times of distress than most any other action.

Generally, preferred stock is issued with an annual dividend expressed in percentage terms. For example, if XYZ Corporation issues a new preferred stock, the notice of issuance is likely to be announced as:

> *"XYZ Corporation announces the issuance of a new Series B 7.375% preferred stock at $25 par value..."*

In this example, new shares are being offered at $25 per share. The annual dividend of 7.375% equates to $1.84375 per share. As most preferred shares remit dividends quarterly, that amounts to anticipated payments of $0.4609375 per share every three months.

THE CAPITAL STRUCTURE

Preferred shares also find preference in the capital structure. Preferred stock is given priority over common shareholders in claims against the assets of a corporation, although they remain subordinate to bondholders. In the event of a liquidation, or other situation in which claims against the corporation's assets are brought forward, the capital structure generally falls as follows:

Removal of assets subject to title arrangements

Liquidator's Costs & Expenses

Creditors with fixed charge over specific assets

Costs & Expenses incurred by the Administrator

Amounts owed to Employees for wages

Amounts owed to Employees for superannuation (i.e. pension contributions)

Payments in respect of worker's injuries

Amounts owed to employees for leave

Retrenchment payments owed to Employees

Senior Bondholders

Bondholders

Preferred Stockholders

Common Stockholders

Historically, investors found comfort in the hierarchy of claims over common stock. A long held belief was that in the worst case scenario of dissolution and/or liquidation that shareholders would be remunerated by the value of the corporation's assets. Even though preferred shareholders were only senior to common shareholders, there was expectation that this position in the capital structure would mitigate loss. In the modern area, where firms are leveraged and litigation is robust, it is unlikely that preferred shareholders stand to benefit during a liquidation at all. The Financial Crisis of 2008 resulted in the bankruptcy of many public companies, and rarely did shareholders (preferred or common) receive much if anything. In fact, the Federal Government's TARP program either fully wiped out some bank preferred series or unilaterally required their conversion into newly minted common shares. While the senior position in the capital structure exists, investors should not embrace a false sense of security that such situation places a floor on bankruptcy exposure.

Types of Preferred Stock

There are several types of preferred stocks. Some of which are actually quite sophisticated and complicated investments, and others are actually not preferred stock at all but simply presented as such since they carry similar characteristics. Prior to exploring some of these related securities, the single greatest differentiator for actual preferred stock that concerns the individual investor is Cumulative v. Non-Cumulative shares.

This seemingly small difference in the issuance is actually quite substantial. As mentioned previously, it is possible that an issuer may not have made all anticipated dividend payments. Cumulative shares require that should a corporation fail to make a dividend payment that any missed payment is to be paid at a future date. Any dividend not paid on time has "passed" and passed dividends are cumulatively referred to dividends in arrears.

A Non-Cumulative, or Straight preferred, simply does not carry this covenant. In the event that a dividend is missed on a non-cumulative issue, that dividend is not passed, but missed. In the event that the dividend is not declared and paid on schedule, that dividend is lost and no obligation on the part of the issuer to make it up exists. Therefore, cumulative preferred stock offer a greater degree of certainty to the investor as not only is there some comfort in the belief that a missed dividend might be made up, but the cumulative missed dividends become part of the investor's claim against the corporation's assets in a liquidation event.

Most basic preferred stock can be differentiated by whether or not they are cumulative. Beyond this, there are a number of other varieties of preferred stock. Among them are:

· ADJUSTABLE RATE PREFERRED STOCK

Sometimes also referred to as Floating Rate Preferred Stock, the dividend is not static. It is based on some index, benchmark or other factors that permit for fluctuating dividends. Often floating rate shares will be benchmark plus a percentage – such as 3 month LIBOR + 0.75%, but also include a minimum dividend rate (i.e. 4%) to entice investors.

· PRIOR PREFERRED STOCK

Many corporations have multiple issues of preferred stock – usually issued at various times over many years. One may be issued with a highest priority designation. In the event that a corporation does not intend to make the dividend payments on all outstanding preferred shares, the prior preferred will be paid first. By default, this makes the prior preferred of an issuer a lower risk than any other preferred stock series that may be outstanding.

· PREFERENCE PREFERRED STOCK

On a basis of seniority, this is the series of preferred issuance from any corporation that ranks immediately behind Prior Preferred stock. The preference preferred will rank above all other issues of preferred stock for order of payments (barring the prior preferred). A corporation may issue multiple series of preference preferred stock, requiring that the security be noted which order it falls in the seniority ladder.

· PUTABLE PREFERRED STOCK

These issues have a Put option that allows the holder (owner) of the security to "put" the security to the issuer under specific circumstances. When putting the shares to the issuer, the owner of the security is effectively forcing the corporation to buy back the shares at par value.

· CONVERTIBLE PREFERRED STOCK

Other than straight preferred shares, convertible preferred stock is a very common security. These shares allow the holder to exchange ("convert") the preferred holdings for a predetermined number of the corporation's common shares. The right to convert may be contingent on specific events, but generally is at the discretion of the holder. While the right to convert is likely non contingent on the market price of the common stock, the conversion rate and market price will determine whether or not conversion is a prudent choice for the investor.

The option to convert is a one-time option. The holder does not have the right to convert back to preferred shares once the conversion option has been exercised.

Investors should fully review the prospectus for any convertible preferred shares as the conversion rights may be contingent upon specific events. Further, while generally the option of the holder, some securities do allow the issuer to force conversion based on specific events. For example, a preferred stock issued by Alexandria Real Estate Equities (Series D Cumulative Convertible Preferred Stock – ticker: AREEP) allows the corporation to force conversion should the price of the common stock exceed 150% of the conversion price for 20 of any 30 consecutive trading days. An investor should always fully understand what they are buying, especially with exceptional caveats such as these.

The average investor with a focus on income generation is not likely to invest in convertible preferred shares. Their focus will likely be on straight preferred shares where they are afforded a high degree of certainty regarding their dividends. However, given the number of convertible preferred stocks in the marketplace, further explanation is warranted. The following example should support the motivation that some investors may have to acquire these securities:

XYZ Corporation Series-A Convertible Preferred Stock pays a 5% dividend. A $25 par value preferred, which equates to a $1.25 annual dividend. The security is non-cumulative and perpetual. The conversion option allows the holder to exchange each share of the preferred for 3 shares of common stock, and is exercisable by the holder at any time. The market price of the preferred shares are $25.

The first element that an investor should recognize is that the security, since it is trading at par value, carries a current yield of 5%. As the issuer does not hold the right to force conversion, the conversion option is something of a lottery ticket for the shareholder since it does not impact the dividend and simply provides an opportunity for the investor to "cash in" on a rise in the common stock.

Whether or not the investor would choose to exercise the conversion option is almost entirely dependent on the market price of the common stock. Since the conversion rate is 3:1 (3 shares of common stock for each share of preferred stock), the equivalent principal value is when the market price of the common stock is exactly 1/3 of the market price of the preferred shares. This is referred to as parity value. The price of the common stock at parity value is known as the conversion price.

100 shares of XYZ Series-A Preferred at $25 = $2,500 market value

100 shares of XYZ Series-A Preferred is convertible into 300 shares of XYZ common stock

$2,500 / 300 shares = $8.33 per share

At any time that the common stock trades above 1/3 of the market price of the preferred stock, there is technically an arbitrage scenario. An arbitrageur may look for pricing discrepancies to take advantage of a situation in which they can purchase the preferred shares, exercise the conversion option and sell the common stock to obtain a risk-free profit. While these situations may exist, they are uncommon and the price discrepancy is exceedingly modest. In an efficient market, the market value of the preferred shares will be effected by the value of the conversion option. This is known as the conversion premium.

For example, when the price of the common stock is below the conversion price, the preferred share's market price is likely based on the fact that it is a 5% fixed-income security (of a certain credit quality). As the price of the common stock rises, the market price of the preferred stock will also rise to maintain equity with the conversion price. If fact, it is more common that the preferred shares will continue to price higher than the conversion price as the preferred shares are effectively 3 shares of the common stock plus a $1.25 dividend.

In this scenario, there is little need to convert the shares to achieve capital gain as the preferred shares have risen as well. In the event that the common stock price rises substantially, then the concern to the investor becomes the possibility that the common stock price will drop. For example, assume that the common stock price rises to $18 in our example above. The market price of the preferred shares is likely $54 or greater. (See below.)

$$1 \text{ preferred share} = 3 \text{ common shares}$$

$$1 \text{ common share} = \$18$$

$$3 \text{ common shares} = \$54$$

The need for the investor to convert is exceedingly small (at least in this example), as the market price of the preferred shares will track appreciation in the common stock. The preferred shares will also carry the stated dividend and continue to rank higher than the common shares in the capital structure. Accordingly, there is notable value to the shareholder. For this reason, convertible preferred stock is generally issued with dividend rates well below what the corporation might have to offer to raise capital without the conversion option. In our example above, the convertible preferred stock was issued with a 5% dividend rate. Perhaps without the conversion option, XYZ Corporation may have had to offer a 6% or 7% dividend rate to attract investors.

In order for an investor to determine the attractiveness of the conversion option, the conversion premium must be considered. The conversion premium is the amount by which the value of the preferred security exceeds the value of the common stock were it converted. Often, at the time of issue, convertible preferred stock is issued with a conversion rate significantly above the then market price of the preferred stock. In continuing with our same example security with a 3:1 conversion rate, let us further assume that at the time of issuance that the common stock traded at $6. The conversion value is $18 (3 x $6), and the preferred market value is $25. The conversion premium is $7, or 28%. [($25-$18)/$25]

Another perspective on this matter would be to recognize that the common stock must appreciate almost 40% to approach parity. Without reasonable expectations for growth and corresponding price appreciation, there is little value to the conversion for the investor. Accordingly, we find that as conversion premiums grow (i.e. the more a common stock must appreciate to approach conversion parity) the more the preferred shares will trade like a debt security – dependent upon its relative dividend rate and credit quality. As premiums shrink to $0, the market price of the preferred shares will trade more in sync with the price of the common shares.

Convertible preferred stock may also be issued to a select investor class in an attempt for a corporation to prevent a hostile takeover. Sometimes referred to as a "poison pill," it is a step a corporate board may take that would discourage outside parties from attempting to acquire a majority of common stock and effect change of management control.

Essentially, the corporation can issue shares of a preferred stock that is convertible into a large number of common shares. Each share of common stock generally holds one vote. An outside party may attempt to acquire greater than 50% of the common stock to hold majority voting rights. A board may issue convertible preferred shares with large enough conversion ratios such that conversion will preclude any outside party from having the opportunity to control a majority of common stock. In this instance, the preferred shares may only be convertible after a single entity gains control over a specified amount of common stock.

In addition to the basic forms of preferred stock described thus far, there are a number of securities that are cumulatively referred to as preferred stock – although they are quite different and not actually preferred stock at all. Most any exchange traded fixed-income security is seemingly lumped together as "preferred" stock; however, quite often the security is actually straight debt. In some cases, this presents the opportunity for an investor to move up the ladder of the capital structure, while maintaining exchange traded liquidity and price availability and quarterly income. When evaluating "preferred" securities, investors should understand the following:

· PINEs (Public Income Notes)

· QUIBs (Quarterly Interest Bonds)

· QUIDs (Quarterly Income Debt Securities)

All of these securities are simply debt that is traded on an exchange like stock, or as they are conjoined, preferred stock. Essentially, these securities are Exchange Traded Debt Securities. They may also carry names such as PETs (Preferred Equity Traded) Bonds. Despite the moniker, they are simply debentures, notes or bonds that trade like stocks. Since they are often priced at $25 par value, rather than industry standard $1,000 par value for bonds, it is easy to understand how they become confused with preferred stock. Nonetheless, as debt, they do rank senior to preferred shares in the capital structure, and the payments are income (not dividends) even if they appear to be the same type of security.

The final security that is lumped with preferred stock are known as Trust Preferred Securities. Rather than issuing preferred stock directly to outside investors (the public or other institutions), a corporation establishes a special trust that buys debt of the issuer and issues preferred stock of the trust to outside investors. This course of issuance presents certain income tax advantages to the issuer, but not to the shareholder. They are taxed like debt obligations, but treated like equity on a company's accounting statements.

More importantly, the trust document generally allows the deferral of payments to shareholders without being considered a default. This became an exceedingly common form of issuance following the Financial Crisis of 2008 by financial institutions as they could defer payments for up to 10 years in some cases. Further, they were treated as Tier-1 capital, rather than liabilities under then banking regulations, making the institution appear better capitalized for regulatory purposes.

It should be no surprise that TRuPs appear to be something of a shell game that provides unreasonable advantages to financial institutions. The Collins Amendment of the Dodd-Frank Act included a provision that excluded TRuPs from the regulatory capital of bank holding companies. Although it included several exemptions for smaller institutions to allow for transition into compliance with the law, consideration as Tier-1 capital was to be phased out by January 2016. There are far less in the market and no longer represent a better alternative for financial institutions to issue in lieu of traditional preferred securities.

Yield

Although preferred shares are a class of stock, and therefore a form of equity, they are far more akin to bonds in practice than common stock. Like a bond that has a coupon rate, preferred stock is issued with a stated dividend rate that is not subject to discretionary revision of the corporation's board of directors. In this way, despite technically being a class of stock, preferred shares are considered a fixed-income security. While some preferreds may be issued with a variable coupon, most are issued with a stated dividend rate. As such, an investor recognizes the yield on their investment in similar vein to investing in debt.

As investors view preferred shares in much the same way as a debt security, the most common, relative factor associated with preferred shares of comparable credit quality is yield. The stated dividend is what the investor will receive in payments from the corporation in payments, but that figure is only meaningful to an investor when coupled with the cost of investment.

Newly issued preferred stock are presented to the market at Par. Par value is the stated face value of any security in the corporate charter. For the purpose of investing, it is both the issue price as well as the redemption value by the issuer for maturity or call purposes. While there is no regulations that require specific par values, most preferred shares are issued with a $25 par value. It is not uncommon for some preferreds to be issued at $50. While far less common, there are some preferreds that have been issued at $100 and even $1,000.

A newly issued preferred will also carry a stated dividend in most cases. For example, a newly issued preferred may carry a $2 annual dividend. An investor will then recognize that the yield on this security, assuming purchase at $25 par value, to be 8%. Much like evaluating any fixed income or debt investment, yield is a fairly general term. To be more specific in evaluating these securities, there are a number of "yields" that should be calculated:

CURRENT YIELD

Current yield is simply dividing the dividend rate by the market price. To utilize our example above of a $2 dividend, $25 par security, the current yield is 8%. Assuming that the security is purchased at some other price, the current yield changes. For example, acquiring the security at a discount to par will result in greater yield. Were an investor able to acquire the preferred at $23, the current yield would be 8.7%. Conversely, were the security be trading at a premium, $27 for example, the yield would decrease to 7.4%. Current yield is a common means of comparing income streams amongst fixed income securities.

YIELD TO MATURITY

Yield to Maturity takes into consideration the annualized yield assuming that the issuer pays back the face value at some point in the future. This is the primary method of evaluating bond investment, as an investor receives periodic interest payments and face value on the maturity date. Securities acquired at a discount will result in a yield to maturity greater than current yield as there will be some additional yield received via a capital repayment in excess of the capital investment.

For example, were an investor to acquire our example security for $24, the investor receives $2 per annum in dividend payments and the $25 face value at maturity – which results in a $1 gain above investment. The longer the time horizon to maturity, the lower the net yield on the difference between investment cost and face value.

Conversely, paying a premium over par value will result in a "loss" of investment value relative to repayment of face value at maturity. However, the cumulative payment streams may not only present a positive return on investment, but an attractive investment overall. Bonds and preferreds are acquired at premiums to face value routinely. An example of such a situation might be purchasing our example security at $27. While the investor will "lose" $2 when the security matures ($25 par value payment less the $27 actual investment), the investor still receives the $2 annual dividend payments over the security's lifetime. Assuming quarterly dividend payments of $0.50 (most preferred shares pay quarterly), and a 10 year to maturity time horizon, the investor's yield to maturity is 6.89%. This may still represent an attractive alternative depending on current market factors.

YIELD TO CALL

Yield to Call is very similar to Yield to Maturity – just more of a "What If" factor. A call is the option of the issuer to call away, or take, the security back from the investor. In most cases, the issuer will pay face value, although some call options require the issuer to pay a modest premium. While evaluating the security, understanding the yield should the security be called is of concern to an investor. The case in which it is of the most concern is when acquiring the security at a premium. In reviewing our last example, suppose that in addition to the 10 year maturity, the issuer has the right to call the security in 6 months at par. Paying $27 for the security may result in positive yield to maturity; however, there is a negative yield to call. Should the security be called in 6 months, the investor will have received ½ year's dividends (totaling $1 in our example) and receive $25 par value. Having spent $27 to acquire the security will result in a cumulative loss of $1, or 3.7%. [$25 par + $1 dividends - $27 purchase price.]

The call is an option of the issuer, and therefore, not guaranteed to occur. Further, the issuer may choose to call on some of the outstanding security – known as a partial call. Circumstances may exist in which an investor is willing to take the chance that the issuer will not exercise their call option. It is simply one other yield factor than an investor must consider prior to deploying capital.

It should be noted not all preferred shares have stated maturities. As many financial companies have been historically able to raise capital with preferred issuance, there was little value to obligating the issuer to eventually repay the issue. Further, as the Federal Reserve embarked on a Quantitative Easing program following the Financial Crisis and Great Recession, a long period of historically low interest rates prevailed. As corporations were able to issue preferred shares with historically low dividend rates, it did not behoove the issuer to intend to repay the capital. Accordingly, investors will find a considerable number of preferred shares in the market that have no maturity. A preferred stock with no maturity date is known as a perpetual security.

Similarly, the value of a call provision to the issuer has grown. It generally does not cost the issuer anything to have the right to call the security in the future, so issuers have taken the opportunity to include call provisions on most preferred issuance. While some calls are at premiums to face value, generally all new issue preferred stock allows the issuer to call the security for par value five years from the date of issue.

The last element of yield that requires mentioning is the inverse relationship between price and yield. This may seem a complicated economic theorem, but it is a rather intuitive and simple to understand reality about risk and return. As prices go up, yields go down – and vice versa. It is most easily illustrated in the following example:

> XYZ Corporation's Series-A 6% Preferred Stock was issued at $25 par value. Over the next few years, interest rates have dropped such that XYZ was able to issue a new Series-B Preferred identical in all respects to its Series-A Preferred, but with a 5% dividend. Clearly, no rational investor would choose the 5% preferred over the 6% preferred if they both traded at $25. If prevailing rates cause these securities to trade for 5% yields, than the original Series-A Preferred is likely trading at $30. ($25 x 6% = $1.50. $1.50/5% = $30.)

> Consequently, the reverse is also true. Assume that rather than a decrease in interest rates since the issue of the Series-A Preferred that rates actually increased such that the Series-B Preferred came to market at 7%. Under these circumstances, the Series-A Preferred is likely to trade at $21.43. ($25 x 6% = $1.50. $1.50/7% = $21.43.)

The inverse relationship between price and yield needs to be understood by anyone who may choose to invest in any fixed rate security. Fairly modest changes in yield can result in significant dollar denominated changes in price.

Risks of Ownership

There are risks with investing in any security. Basic investing theory stipulates that any return over the risk-free rate (generally read as U.S. T-Bills) is derived from the risk accepted by making the investment. Investing in preferred stock is no different. While preferred shares tend to be far less volatile than common equity shares, as they are more akin to debt, does not mean that they are a riskless class of security. The primary risks that any investor should be aware of are as follows:

DEFAULT RISK

Technically, the non-payment of a preferred share dividend is not a default, but it is a far easier term to grasp and effectively conveys this prominent risk. As dividends are paid at the discretionary of the corporation's board of directors, they may suspend preferred stock dividends at any time. As most investors purchase preferred stock exclusively for the income stream afforded by the stated dividends, there is little value to a preferred that is not paying dividends – particularly non-cumulative shares.

In the event that a corporation suspends a preferred stock dividend, shareholders are almost certain to witness a market value drop in the share price. In a non-cumulative issue, where the business is clearly struggling, market participants may believe that the dividend is unlikely to be resumed and find demand for the shares evaporate quickly. That may result in share price to be quite low. In fact, finding a lack of buyers could result in an illiquid security that cannot be sold. In other terms, even if temporarily, it may become worthless.

In the case of a cumulative preferred, there is a greater chance of retained value as missed dividends accrue. Of course, if similar circumstances exist (where the market does not believe that the dividend will be reinstated), it is possible that the security trades as worthless as mentioned above. Being a cumulative share does not cause the share price to trade for accrued dividend value.

An investor should recognize that suspension of a dividend is not termination of the security. That is, a corporation's decision to suspend the dividend does not remove the preferred shares from an investor's account or cause the security to no longer be listed on an exchange. That is a fairly important detail as the corporation may not make dividend payments on common shares, or further junior preferred shares, so long as dividends on the preferred are suspended. Most issuers of preferred stock are in the financial (banking and insurance), real estate (REIT) and utility industries. These industries' common stocks historically remit common stock dividends, and are keen to do so to attract common shareholders. (Some mutual funds can only buy stocks of companies that pay dividends.) Therefore, the suspension of the dividend may be a temporary measure. Investors should also note that dividend suspension is a serious situation and is almost certainly indicative of fundamental or structural problems within the corporation.

Suspension of the common stock dividend can be greeted by the market as a wise move if the corporation is under financial stress. Such an action adds to cashflow and provides more certainty of the issuer meeting debt obligations. While not technically a default, suspension or deferral of dividend payments on preferred shares is largely treated by the market as one in the same. Corporations and their advisers are keenly aware of this fact. It is generally understood that suspension of preferred dividend payments is akin to default on a debt and will cause the corporation greater difficulty in dealing with creditors or obtaining access to additional capital. While it does occur, this market perception results in most issuers to be quite hesitant to do so.

INSOLVENCY RISK

In many ways, Insolvency Risk is Default Risk on steroids. Insolvency occurs when a creditor is unable to satisfy their financial obligations. Dividend suspension may be a course of action that a corporation chooses to take, whereas insolvency is the instance in which the corporation has no choice – they simply do not have the funds to meet their obligations. While there are legal differences, an investor can consider this circumstance the same as the risk of bankruptcy.

Whether the insolvency is technical or actual is not of concern when understanding the risk. The risk that the investor faces is that the issuer will not make any additional payments, dividends or principal, on the preferred shares. In the case of insolvency or bankruptcy, it is almost certain that the preferred share's market value will be inherently worthless. It is unlikely that an investor would find a willing buyer for their shares and therefore will attempt to write them off as a complete capital loss.

Insolvency or bankruptcy then references the preferred shareholder's rank in the capital structure. Being senior to common shareholders, and potentially first among other preferred series shares, has historically lent some comfort to investors in this worst case scenario. While this might be accurate and legitimate in the private sector, investors in publicly traded securities should be cautioned that claims against the corporation usually settle with no compensation. Preferred shareholders generally fall low enough in the pecking order that little or nothing is left of corporate assets. In fact, in the event of bankruptcy, shareholders are more likely to be compensated just a few pennies per share through class action litigation. Investors should recognize that in the event of insolvency or bankruptcy that their investment is a complete loss.

CREDIT RISK

Many preferred shares will carry a ratings agency rating, such as from S&P or Moody's. That is one generally accepted measure of credit quality, but investors must always take care to conduct their own due diligence on an issuer to fully understand the quality of what they are buying. Many preferred shares will carry a different ratings agency rating than the firm's debt. Generally, preferred shares will be rated one or two tiers below the corporation's debt since there are less guarantees associated with the payment of dividends when compared to the payment of bond interest.

Credit risk is not the same as default risk, although it is an indicator of it. Credit risk, when thinking of fixed income, is the risk that an issuer will default on their obligations. When thinking of preferred shares, investors should be more concerned with the risk to share price associated with credit quality changes when contemplating credit risk.

Essentially, this risk is the chance that the credit quality of the issuer will deteriorate. Changes in credit quality will be reflected in the market price.

A 5% preferred security that is rated 'AA' will trade at a higher price than 5% security rated 'B.' Deteriorating credit quality raises the risk of dividend suspension, which in turn will cause investors to demand a greater rate of return (or yield) in order to accept the increased risk. As the dividend is a fixed amount, the means by which to obtain a higher yield is price erosion. Recall - there is an inverse relationship between price and yield.

LIQUIDITY RISK

The preferred stock market is many times smaller than the debt market, and far fewer shares are traded than for an issuer's common stock. It is not uncommon for the preferred shares of some major issuers to trade as little as a few hundred shares per day. This lack of volume also has a tendency to see greater spreads between the bid and ask for the average security. Such circumstances can make it more difficult to buy or sell a specific preferred issue at a reasonable price. This is particularly onerous for larger investors or small institutions who may need days to liquidate a security to avoid significant impact on market price. Light trading volumes of secondary market securities should be noted prior to deciding to invest in a specific issue.

INTEREST RATE RISK

This is the single largest risk that a shareholder will face when investing in preferred stocks because over the long term it is unavoidable. Beyond the issuing corporation's financial strength and stability, prevailing interest rates are likely to have the greatest impact on market price. Recall that there is an inverse relationship between price and yield.

Interest Rate Risk will have a greater impact on perpetual preferred stock than those with stated maturities. The simple reason being that an investor can calculate their yield to maturity on any security that has a defined end date. In these instances, the preferred shares are more likely to trade like equivalent bonds of similar maturity as opposed to simply the current yield of the security. Similarly, the longer the time to maturity, the greater the impact on price.

A parallel to interest rate risk is the risk of coupon resets on adjustable rate securities. In the case of Adjustable Rate Preferred Stock, the dividend rate is generally set as a benchmark interest rate plus or minus a spread. For example, 3 month LIBOR plus 2.0%. While many adjustable rate preferred shares will include some minimum dividend figure to entice investors, there exists a chance that the dividend will decrease based on market factors effecting the underlying benchmark rate.

For example, immediately following the Financial Crisis of 2008, interest rates plummeted around the globe as central banks scrambled to protect economic growth. 3 Month LIBOR dropped from 4.7% at the start of 2008 to below 0.25% in 2013. A preferred with the example characteristics above, would have seen the dividend rate go from 6.7% to 2.25% (assuming no dividend floor) over that time. Dropping rates across all fixed-income securities may have allowed the market price to remain relatively static; however, the investor's yield and dollar denominated income has taken a considerable hit.

There reverse situation, in which interest rates rise, would seem to be a boon for investors and not a risk. To a certain extent this is true, as rising interest rates will result in a rising dividend rate on the preferred share resulting in increased income to the investor. As there is an inverse relationship between price and yield, the rising dividend rate will also likely protect the preferred share's market price from depreciating as one would expect with a fixed rate security. The risk, however, is embedded in the fact that the corporate issuer now has a larger payment obligation. As the issuing firm's financial obligations rise, there exists increasing risks to credit quality, dividend suspension and ultimately the firm's solvency. It can be a case of "be careful what you wish for...you just might get it."

CALL RISK

Quite simply, Call Risk is the risk that the preferred will be called by the issuer and the shareholder receive cash. In some cases, an investor may hope that the issuer calls the security – as in the case when an investor acquired the security at substantial discount to par and would receive a capital gain. In most cases, an issuer will call a preferred stock if interest rates have dropped. Much like a homeowner choosing to refinance their mortgage when rates have dropped, a corporation may choose to refinance their preferred obligations (just like their debt obligations) at lower rates. In this case, calling a preferred presents the shareholder with two specific risks:

Reinvestment Risk – where the shareholder is faced with the prospect of reinvesting the proceeds of the called security at the prevailing market rates. If rates have dropped, it is likely that the investor will have to reinvest the call proceeds at lower rates than they had been previously invested.

Risk of Principal Loss – where the shareholder incurs a loss as a result of the preferred stock being called. If an investor acquired the shares are a premium to par value, he/she then would receive less in principal from the call than their initial investment. This may not represent a net negative return on investment, but it will result in a lower yield than the current yield at time of investment.

Similarly, as interest rates drop, the price of fixed income securities rise (recall the inverse relationship again). Accordingly, the market price of the shareholder's preferred stock is likely higher than par value, or at least higher than investment price if rates have declined notably since that time. At the announcement of the call, the market price of the preferred shares will almost immediately trade just below the cumulative value of the call price plus any remaining dividends to be paid. (Any other price would present an arbitrage opportunity.) Regardless if the call price is higher or lower than the investor's cost basis, the call could result in sudden, and potentially substantial, drops in market value which could impact portfolio value. Perhaps it is nothing more than paper loss, but imagine having $56,000 in a position at 10:00 a.m. that trades at $50,200 at noon due to call announcement! It has happened before. It will undoubtedly happen again. A large portfolio of preferred stock remains exposed to notable principal impact in a decreasing interest rate environment due to issuer calls.

28

Tax Considerations

From a tax perspective, not all preferred stocks are created equal. For tax purposes, dividends are either considered "Qualified" or "Non-Qualified." If a dividend is considered qualified, they are tax-free for those in the 10% and 15% brackets (to the extent that the dividend income remains within those brackets). They are taxed at 15% for those in the 25% - 35% brackets, and taxed at 20% for those whose income is great enough to eclipse the 35% bracket. Non-qualified dividends are taxed as ordinary income.

Most preferred issues will inform the investor if the security qualifies for reduced tax treatment. While it may be difficult to discern the difference without assistance, the rationale for reduced tax treatment is rooted in the taxation of corporations. Corporations are not permitted to deduct dividends prior to determining their tax liability. Therefore, dividends paid by corporations (be they on preferred or common stock) are paid with the corporation's after-tax dollars. Were an investor to then pay full income tax on those dividends, the same income would be fully taxed twice. (Of course, it is still double taxed albeit not _fully_ double taxed.) Hybrid preferred securities carry characteristics of both equity and debt, and debt service is paid pre-tax by a corporation. Therefore those funds which are paid to investors with a corporation's pre-tax dollars are subjected to full, ordinary income taxation by the investor.

To further complicate an investor's tax situation, there is a holding period requirement for qualifying preferred stock dividends. In order for shareholders of preferred stock to qualify for the qualified treatment of dividends received, the investor must hold the security for at least 90 days after receipt of the dividend (including the ex-dividend date). This treatment is then, therefore, _per dividend_, and not per security. Tax treatment of each dividend received on a qualifying preferred issue will be based on the holding period after receipt of said dividend.

Preferred stock, like any equity security, is subjected to capital gains taxation when sold. In the event that a preferred issue is called or matures, the resulting proceeds less the original cost basis (original investment amount) represents the net capital gain or loss. If an investor finds the opportunity to acquire shares of a preferred stock at a discount to par value, and the security is subsequently called for par, the difference is a capital gain. While the resulting tax consideration is not often a significant factor in the investor's decision making, it is something of which investors should be aware.

Corporations receive special tax treatment of their investment in other corporation's preferred stock. In most cases, corporations are entitled to a dividend received deduction that allows them to exclude 70% of dividend income from their taxable income. This has created a situation in which corporations are actually the largest holder of preferred stock.

AFTER-TAX YIELD

It should be noted that investors should be concerned with just how much money an investment returns after all expenses – including commissions, fees and taxes. Without delving into a dissertation about tax advantaged investing, any fixed income investor should understand After-Tax Yield. After all, in the end it's not about how much you get…it's how much you keep.

The gross yield on a security is the yield an investor generates from dividends or interest payments, but the after-tax yield is what the investor receives after they remit taxes on the income received from the security. Put simply, it is merely incorporating the tax liability from investment income into the final calculation of return on said investment. Clearly, the higher the tax bracket, the higher the taxes due and, in turn, the lower the after-tax yield. Therefore, securities with lower tax liability result in relatively higher after-tax yield to investors in higher tax brackets. Consider the following example:

XYZ Series A Preferred Stock pays a $2 annual dividend. The security is acquired at $25 par. The yield to an investor is 8% ($2/$25). An investor in the 40% tax bracket will owe 40% of the income received as tax, or $0.80 ($2 x 40%). The investor's net income is then only $1.20 ($2 - $0.80), and their after tax yield is 4.8% ($1.20/$25).

If the investor were in a 30% tax bracket, their after-tax yield is 5.6%. It should be intuitive that since the investor has a lower tax liability (30% as opposed to 40%) that they will then pay less tax and walk away with greater net return. Accordingly, the lower tax bracket results in a greater after-tax return.

If we now are told that the XYZ Series A Preferred in our example is a qualifying dividend security, then the example investor above in the 40% tax bracket actually only has a 20% tax liability on the dividend income received. Therefore, rather than a $0.80 tax liability on the $2 dividend, the tax liability is only $0.40. Accordingly, the after tax yield is now actually 6.4% [($2-$0.40)/$25]. It also improves the net after-tax yield of our investor in the 30% bracket, as their tax liability would decrease to 15% for a qualified preferred. Clearly, preferred stock with qualified dividends provides net return advantages when considering tax liability, particularly to those in higher tax brackets.

The after-tax yield also allows an investor to compare the net returns of one investment versus another should they have differing tax liabilities. By calculating the net after-tax yields on potential investments, the investor may determine which security will result in the greatest after tax returns – even if the gross yields appear otherwise. Consider the following example for an investor in the 40% tax bracket:

Security A: $2 dividend, $25 par value with a qualified dividend

Security B: $2.40 dividend, $25 par value that is not qualified

Security A is identical to our previous example, and the investor in the 40% tax bracket has a 6.4% after tax yield. Security B's after tax yield is:

$$\$2.40 \times 40\% \text{ tax} = \$0.96 \text{ tax liability}$$

$$\text{Net income} = \$2.40 - \$0.96 = \$1.44$$

$$\text{After Tax Yield} = \$1.44/\$25 = 5.76\%$$

31

Although Security B carries a dividend that is 20% greater than Security A, it will actually produce lower net returns for the investor given the tax liability. At first glance, all other concerns being equal, an investor would be naturally drawn to Security B given the substantially higher dividend rate; however, it actually results in lower net yield once an astute investor considers the tax implications.

ETFs & CEFs

EXCHANGE TRADED FUND

Since the early 2000's the rise of Exchange Traded Funds (ETFs) has been rather meteoric. A less expensive, or potentially more focused, version of a mutual fund has had great appeal to investors and sponsors alike. As the ETF marketplace grew, the number of funds focusing on narrow investment opportunities exploded. Today there are ETFs that allow investors to speculate on 3x the change in the Euro versus the Dollar or the daily price change of a commodity basket. There are also quite a few ETFs that focus on a portfolio of preferred stock.

At first glance, holding a portfolio of preferred stocks becomes an attractive alternative to acquiring individual issues. Clearly, the opportunity for diversification is great. Rather than acquiring shares of a few individual issues, investment in an ETF provides a portfolio of perhaps 50, or even, 100 different securities. This will substantially reduce the investor's default and credit risk, as any individual issuer and/or security does not likely represent a substantial portion of the overall portfolio. While some ETFs may offer the investor to focus specifically on REITs or the Financial sector, which would in turn result in sector specific risk, there are many that provide investors exposure across industries for full diversification.

In most cases, preferred stock ETFs will remit dividends on a monthly basis. This is particularly attractive to investors looking to generate income. Increased frequency of cashflow aids in this objective. ETFs will also attract more investors than the average individual issue, which will aid in liquidity. This will make it much easier for an investor to move in and/or out of a position without much consideration to doing so at a fair price.

The other primary driver that many investors find attractive about deploying capital via ETFs rather than individual issues is that the ETF employs a team of professionals who conduct due diligence on the securities and their issuers. Most individual investors do not have the time, knowledge or resources to fully analyze the credit quality of an issuer. Relying exclusively on rating agency ratings, or issuer name recognition, is insufficient risk assessment which may in turn result in adverse consequences. Much like a bond, issuer insolvency will generally result in a total loss of capital investment – a much greater risk than the average "safety focused" income investor is knowingly aware of. The management team is generally comprised of credit analysts who are adept at understanding the risks of credit quality. The management fees assessed by most ETF sponsors are also fairly reasonable, generally less than 0.50%.

CLOSED END FUND

A traditional mutual fund is an Open Ended Fund. Each time an investor places capital into the fund, new shares are issued to the investor at Net Asset Value (NAV). Net Asset Value is the value of the underlying portfolio divided by the number of shares outstanding. There is no limit to the number of shares that the fund sponsor will issue, hence the "open ended" nature. The investment is not traded on an exchange, but rather processed by the mutual fund company.

A Closed End Fund is issued with a specific number of shares are launch. If a fund sponsor raises $5,000,000, they may issue 500,000 shares at $10 when the fund begins trading. Much like any other stock, the CEF will list on an exchange where investors can buy and sell during normal trading hours. This provides certain advantages and disadvantages over a traditional, open-end fund.

A mutual fund's NAV is determined at the close of business each day when the closing price for all underlying securities are known. As a CEF can trade intraday (shares may be bought and sold during normal market hours), the fund's NAV is difficult to ascertain from one moment to the next. Even in the advance technological age, knowing precisely the NAV is difficult given the positions may be traded by management, etc. Beyond the difficultly in calculating NAV intraday, since the number of shares is fixed, the market price is subject to supply and demand similar to any other exchange traded security. Even if the NAV is $10, a lack of buyers may preclude sale at that price. Similarly, a lack of sellers may necessitate that a buyer pay more than NAV for shares.

This pricing discrepancies above or below NAV are known as Premium or Discount, respectively. The risk to an investor is that he/she may have to transact at prices away from the genuine value of the security's underlying portfolio. While this is indeed properly characterized as a risk, it also potentially represents an opportunity as well. Let us examine the following two perspectives on the same scenario:

XYZ Preferred Stock CEF has a NAV of $15 per share. It pays a monthly dividend of $0.0625 per share, which equates to a 5% yield. If investors generally expect rates to rise in the near to intermediate term, they may begin to liquidate the fund for fear that the value of the underlying securities may fall. (Recall the inverse relationship between price and yield.) If investors demand a 6% yield to own the security, the market price may drop to $12.50. This would result in a 16.67% discount to NAV. Clearly this is a risk to shareholders.

A prospective investor may look at this CEF and realize that he/she is paying $0.8333 on the dollar for the portfolio. After all, the actual securities that comprise the fund are currently worth $15 (the NAV), and the investor only needs to pay $12.50 to purchase $15 worth of securities. While the market value of the underlying securities may in fact drop in price, that potential, or even likely, drop in price has been factored into the market price of the CEF by the marketplace. Further, the investor is acquiring a 6% yielding security which provides the downside protection against rate increases that the market is anticipating. Effectively, at least some portion of potential rate increases has been hedged by acquiring the shares at a discount to value. Beyond this possible downside protection, should the market perception prove to be incorrect, the discount may narrow resulting in capital appreciation in the share price in addition to the monthly dividend income.

At times an investor may consider acquiring a CEF with the anticipation that market sentiment may drive the share price to a premium. While this is not as common in fixed income investing as it is with equity focused CEFs, it does occur. Anticipations of rate decreases may drive the price of the fund to a premium to NAV. Of course, while price increases will result in capital appreciation, it will also result in declining current yield should dividends remain static.

A notable risk common to ETFs and CEFs is the changing underlying portfolio. As with any individual issue that an investor may own, the holdings within the fund are subject to calls, maturity and default. Over a long enough period of time, the securities comprising the fund will change for any of these reasons, as well as management decisions regarding where to deploy capital. Accordingly, as the securities in the portfolio change so does the income generated. In a declining interest rate environment, the portfolio managers will almost certainly have to reinvest at successively lower rates. Over time, that will likely result in proportionately lower dividend payments.

There are other factors which can impact the fund's declared dividends, such as changing cost of leverage, etc. In the end, what every investor should recognize is that unlike investing in individual preferred stock with stated dividend rates, the dividend rate of a fund is not guaranteed. In fact, they can change quite often thereby reducing the certainty of income an investor will receive. Further, all things being equal, reduced dividend rates will likely result in dropping market share price as well leaving the investor exposed to principal fluctuation. In many ways, this is very similar to investment in bond funds. Given that perpetual preferred have no stated maturity, their infinite duration makes the securities hyper-price sensitive and the most susceptible to changes in interest rates.

Finally, there is also one fairly unique advantage to investing in a CEF or ETF that an investor generally cannot achieve on their own – access to institutional issues. Quite often, a large corporation may issue what they perceive to be a small offering, perhaps $10-$25 million. The cost to bring this issue to market via a syndicate and exchange may prove unattractive, and the issuer may find an advantage to raising the capital directly through institutional investors. An institutional investor may be a mutual fund, hedge fund or other large investor that will take 50-100% of the offering. Therefore, funds may have the opportunity to acquire securities which are otherwise unavailable to the general public through other means, offering greater diversification and other benefits.

There exists yet one more advantage to investment in preferred stock via ETF or CEF than mutual fund of individual issue – the opportunity to employ an options strategy. Some funds are large and popular enough that there is an active options market on the shares. This presents the investor the opportunity to hedge their investment via put options, or engage in a covered call strategy to leverage their income generation. While it is not particularly common, it is yet one more possibility that an investor cannot execute otherwise.

Case Studies

The information contained within this tome should provide a complete narrative of the various types of preferred stock so that any financial advisor or investor can fully understand them. However, having the knowledge to understand preferred stock from beginning to end does not necessarily make investing decisions simple. A decision to invest hard earned capital into a preferred stock, much like any other security, requires that the advisor or investor conduct their due diligence and understand the macroeconomic factors that could impact the market price or sustainability of the underlying security.

It should be noted that this chapter does not provide security analysis, or claim to provide the skills, resources or information necessary to allow any individual or firm to engage in a competent investing decision. Rather, the following case studies of bona fide, real-world securities will provide some anecdotal narrative as to how an investors may view the potential of deploying capital. Just like any security, investors should discuss with the risks and opportunities with their advisors prior to making any investment.

*All studies are in the context of early 2015.

CHESAPEAKE LODGING TRUST
7.75% Series A Cumulative Preferred Stock
Par Value: $25
Ticker: CHSP-A
Exchange: NYSE
Cusip: 165240201
Callable: 7/17/2017 at par
Maturity: None
Distribution Dates: 1/15, 4/15, 7/15 & 10/15

Chesapeake Lodging Trust is a Real Estate Investment Trust. The firm primarily invests in upscale hotels in major business cities. For reference, they operate the Hyatt Regency in Boston and the Hyatt Herald Square in midtown New York City.

What anyone should be able to quickly recognize from the security synopsis provided above is that this is a traditional preferred stock that pays a 7.75% annual dividend in quarterly installments. The preferred is cumulative, and was issued at $25 par value.

From a dividend perspective, 7.75% annual dividend yield equates to annual dividends of $1.9375 per share, or $0.484375 per quarter. The cumulative nature of the dividends should provide some additional comfort to the investor. As it is a traditional preferred stock, the dividends are qualified and taxed at 15% or 20% depending on the individual investor's tax profile.

The issuer has the right to call the security for 7/17/2017. Any investor can they determine their yield to call should they acquire the shares in advance of the call date. Were the security to be purchased at any market price above $25 (which is the call price), the investor's yield would be less than 7.75% were the security to be called – a risk that a potential investor needs to calculate and understand.

Of course, the possibility of a call is not necessarily a reason to avoid the security. Suppose that the investor believes that the shares will be called for 7/17/2017. Perhaps the shares trade at $26.30 (which they did in early March 2015). An investor should recognize the following:

There are 10 dividends due. 3 remaining for 2015 (January already paid), all 4 for 2016 and 3 for 2017 (January, April and the final dividend at call in July). Therefore, total potential dividends through the call date = $4.84375/share.

Total dividends:	$4.84375	
Call Value:	$25.00	
less Investment:	$(26.30)	*market price*
Total Return:	$3.24375	

Assuming that dividends are paid, and they would have to be in order for the security to be called since it is cumulative, the investors stands to profit $3.24 per share over a 28 month holding period. At a $26.30 investment price, this represents a cumulative return of 12.33%. The yield to call, however, is approximately 4.8%.

The context of the investment must be made in the context of the world at large at the time of investment. 4.8% may not seem to be a worthwhile investment for some investors, in which case they may choose to avoid it altogether. Assuming that the dividends are "safe" (otherwise meaning that the investor anticipates that Chesapeake Lodging Trust is unlikely to suspend the dividend), then the yield to call is the minimum return over the investor's holding period barring sale at some lower price. Should the issuer not call the security on 7/17/2017, the investor's yield will continue to climb as successive payments will slowly increase the yield over the investment lifetime towards current yield. In this case, current yield is 7.37%.

Even were an investor to believe that Chesapeake Lodging Trust will call the security, 4.8% for a 28 month holding period may seem to be a worthwhile investment should the short term alternatives available in the market be considerably less. In the context of this case study, 10 year U.S. Treasury rates at this time were 2.2%, and the 2 year rate was 0.63%.

The call is only one of the risks that the investor needs to recognize and appreciate. While this case study does perhaps not adequately provide the reader with appreciation of then current market circumstances, one should recognize that the security is carrying a 7.75% dividend in a 2.2% 10 year Treasury world. The security, when priced at $26.30, carried a current yield of 7.37%. The relative yield is quite a spread over treasuries, and the relatively high yield should give investors as much pause as salivation for opportunity. In summary, high dividend yields can sometimes be an indicator of investor skittishness or financial distress. There is usually a reason why the yields are high.

It would be improper in this case study to attempt to provide full analysis of Chesapeake Lodging Trust; however, some basic financial figures can provide further insight. The issuer had debt outstanding of $552 million, and cash on hand of $29 million at the time. They had a debt-to-equity ratio of 51 times. For liquidation purposes, the book value was $20.08. The income statement did reflect positive free operating cash flow of $119.63 million and leveraged free cash flow of over $93 million.

The common shares carried a dividend of $1.40 per share. There were 53.89 million shares outstanding, which equates to common dividends of more than $75 million per annum. As we understand that no common dividends can be paid should the preferred dividend be suspended, there is a $75 million cushion for the Series A preferred. Further, the Series A preferred was an offering of 4.4 million shares, which means that the preferred dividend represents a cumulative obligation to Chesapeake of only $8,525,000. With free cash flow of $100 million, the preferred dividend does not appear to be financially onerous to the firm.

In order to call the security, Chesapeake would need $110 million to purchase all 4.4 million outstanding shares. That would exceed all cash on the balance sheet by almost 4 times, and require almost all free cashflow. Unless the trust is intent on liquidating a property or holding a secondary offering, there is insufficient resources to call the security. That, of course, does not mean that they cannot "refinance" it with a new issue of preferred stock at a lower interest rate or via a more traditional debt offering; however, given the firm's financials, an expectation of rising interest rates at the time, and the lack of immediate concern regarding the call allowed the yield to remain elevated.

Finally, whether or not an advisor or investor finds this yield either attractive or concerning, one must always consider macroeconomic factors that could affect the corporation. In the end, whether buying common or preferred shares, the investment is in the corporation itself – and the issuer's performance is of utmost concern. Chesapeake Lodging Trust is, in simple terms, a hotel operator. Global economic recession, strengthening U.S. dollar versus foreign currencies and/or increasing air travel costs could all potentially affect the U.S. leisure market. If the prospects for hotels is bleak, then so is likely the prospects for Chesapeake Lodging Trust. No matter how attractive the yield or corporate financials may be, any investor must be forward looking in their assessment of the corporation to understand if their current assessment of the balance sheet and outlook remains favorable under stressful conditions. The risk to the shares is an extension of the risks to the business itself.

HUNTINGTON BANCSHARES
8.50% Series A Non-Cumulative Convertible Preferred Stock

Par Value: $1,000
Ticker: HBANP
Exchange: NGM
Cusip: 446150401
Callable: 4/15/2013 at par
Maturity: None
Distribution Dates: 1/15, 4/15, 7/15 & 10/15

This security was chosen to provide illustration of how complicated it can be to determine whether or not to deploy capital into a convertible preferred stock.

Huntington Bancshares is a regional bank holding company that operates the Huntington National Bank. Much like in our previous case study, one will notice that this is a quarterly paying, traditional preferred stock. In this case, however, the shares are non-cumulative and convertible. The non-cumulative nature of the shares eliminates some confidence that an investor would have in a cumulative share class, but the convertible nature is a large point of focus.

First and foremost, an investor is deploying capital into the corporation. If one does not wish to invest in banks, or more specifically this bank, the preferred share is not an investment worth making. This may perhaps be of even greater concern given the conversion option, as there exists the possibility that the investor may convert into common shares – whether they want to or not.

The involuntary conversion comes from a clause contained in the share's call option. While the option to convert is usually considered something of a lottery ticket option for the holder of the security, this security carried a clause in which the issuer may force conversion under the following circumstances:

> **On or after 4/15/2013, if the price of the common stock exceeds 130% of the conversion price for 20 of any 30 consecutive trading days, the company may, at their option, cause the preferred shares to be converted into common shares at the then prevailing conversion price.**

Let us dissect this situation, which is an option of the issuer. In essence, this provides that if the preferred shares carry a market price that is 30% above the conversion price then the corporation can force the conversion of the shares upon the investor. This is a prime option for the issuer.

At the time, the common share price was approximately $11.00. The conversion option for the shareholder was to convert to 83.668 common shares. (At the time of issue, this was a conversion price of $11.95.) Were an investor to elect to convert at that moment in time, the common shares would be worth $920.34. The preferred shares par value is $1,000, and the security remained callable at par.

Given that the security was already 24 months beyond the initial call date, one might anticipate that the corporation was unlikely to call the security. There were only 500,000 preferred shares issued; however, the $1,000 par value equates to a $500 million price tag to call the entire issue. Of course, they may have the opportunity to "refinance" the relatively high 8.5% dividend, as discussed previously, via new issue preferred stock or debt; however, as the issuer has the option to force conversion if the common shares trade at $15.54 for about a month it may behoove them to simply wait.

The option to force conversion would require a 41% appreciation in the market price of the common shares. While that would be a welcome return for a common share investor, it only requires a 7.02% annualized rate of appreciation for 5 years to occur. If the market price appreciates approximately 12% per year over 3 years, the corporation could be able to force conversion. Rather than exhaust $500 million of corporate resources, or undergo the process of "refinance" via new issues, the board may choose to bide their time and defer to a later date if the entire issue can be effectively swept away into common shares carrying approximately one half the annualized dividend obligation of the preferred share class.

What the board of directions was considering at that time I do not pretend to know. Nor does any potential investor...which is what in turn makes the involuntary conversion a risk. Of course, the risk that one might be forced to convert is only a risk from two perspectives:

First, since the investor can sell the common shares immediately after the conversion, the genuine risk is market value fluctuation. In this case, the conversion would increase the number of outstanding common shares by approximately 20%. Announcement of the intended conversion would almost certainly impact the price of the common shares – perhaps not by as much as the percentage increase in shares outstanding, but a downward impact in share price nonetheless. As this is almost certain to be a rather instantaneous price adjustment, preferred shareholders are likely to experience a market value reduction. Immediate sale of shares after conversion would be a loss versus preannouncement valuation.

The other primary risk to forced conversion is based on the investment cost of purchasing the preferred shares. Herein lies the true difficulty in analyzing this security at the time, as at the time the preferred shares market price was $1,350.

At $1,350, the current yield is 6.3%. Perhaps not a bad yield in the then interest rate environment; however, as the issue was already callable at par, the yield to call is actually negative. Were the security called for 4/15/2015, then the investor who acquired shares at $1,350 just prior would actually lose $328.75 per share, or approximately 25%. That's a sizeable loss, but also indicative of market sentiment that a call is unlikely.

The premium to par value essentially creates a conversion price for the investor that differs for those who may have acquired the shares at issue. As the number of common shares to convert into is held constant (at 83.668), were conversion to occur the new investor needs a $16.14 common share price to be even. Since the investor acquired shares at $1,350, any common share price below $16.14 results in a negative return at the time of conversion. Accordingly, a new investor takes the risk that involuntary conversion would result in at least a temporary loss on capital. Were the corporation not to force conversion (as it does still represent an increase of almost 20% of shares outstanding), the investor requires that the common shares appreciate approximately 47% to be breakeven on a conversion option for the shareholder to exercise.

This particular case study is somewhat exceptional in its complicated nature. Most preferred stock investing is much simpler in its analysis and due diligence. Clearly, this particular issue involved added layers of thought and assumption given the premium to call price and conversion options.

BREITBURN ENERGY PARTNERS
8.25% Series A Cumulative Redeemable Preferred Units

Par Value: $25
Ticker: BBEPP
Exchange: NGS
Cusip: 106776115
Callable: 5/15/2019 at par
Maturity: None
Distribution Dates: 15th of each month

BreitBurn Energy Partners is an independent oil and gas limited partnership which develops oil and natural gas properties in the United States. Much like in our Chesapeake Lodging Trust example, this is a traditional preferred security which is both cumulative and callable. Investors will find some comfort, again, in the cumulative nature of the dividends, and also likely find quite attractive the monthly distribution dates. Once again, the current yield and yield to call are fairly simply to determine based on market price at the time.

The reason I have chosen to highlight this particular security as a case study example has to do with the macroeconomic forces that exhibit influence on any investment. At first glance, this security is rather simple and straightforward as described above. The complicating factor is the fact that the issuer is not only in the energy sector, but a firm that is focused on the development of oil and gas properties. Like all corporations of similar focus, they have notable debt – at the time a debt to equity ratio of almost 90 times! With debt of $3.36 billion and cash on the balance sheet of only $12.6 million, solvency was a legitimate concern. It is an 8.25% preferred for a reason.

The primary macroeconomic factor in this case are commodity prices. More specifically, the price of oil and natural gas. As the price of oil falls, those in the business of producing and selling oil are bound to generate less revenue per unit of output. To place in the proper context, in late 2014 the price of oil began to drop precipitously. In fact, by early 2015 the price of WTI crude oil had dropped from over $100 per barrel to the low $40's. The market price of energy sector common stocks were hit quite hard, and the market price of many preferred shares were impacted as well. Those smaller, exploration/development focused companies such as BreitBurn, were particularly impacted as many market participants expected several of these firms to become insolvent.

In the case of BreitBurn, the preferred shares traded as low as $17.90 in January of 2015. At $18, the current yield was 11.46%, and clearly the yield to call was extraordinary. Whether or not this price drop could be considered "panic" is for individuals to determine for themselves, but the market price did represent an opportunity for many investors to invest at depressed levels. Like any investment, one must analyze the corporation.

The drop in commodity prices certainly would have some impact on the firm; however, the management team had hedged a considerable portion of the firm's production. 75% of all production was priced hedged through 2015, 60+% hedged through 2016 and almost 40% hedged through 2017. Those hedges would provide a greater degree of certainty to the firm's cashflow as it would reduce commodity price volatility on the firm's revenue stream. While commodity prices may remain low, or even go substantially lower in the future, the price hedges would provide some certainty to the preferred dividend for some time. At the time, BrietBurn was continuing to issue common share dividends to the tune of $200 million per year, while the preferred obligation was only $18.375 million per year.

Do not misinterpret the statement above that the discount to par value represented an opportunity for arbitrage or some special circumstance. Prices are generally inefficient in the short term, and astute investors would have realized that BreitBurn Energy was not in eminent threat of bankruptcy due to the crash in oil prices. However, for the intermediate to longer term analysis, low commodity prices, lower than anticipated reserves and/or other business issues (not to exclude possibly poor management) may still render the firm insolvent. The study is meant to highlight the factors and risks that an investor should consider when evaluating the merits of a preferred stock security beyond simply yields and price.

Lastly, another element that is worth mentioning, although it likely does not enter into investor psychology for deployment of capital, is the situation of merger or acquisition. At the time described above, while a sense of panic was not necessarily felt throughout the market, the solvency of small firms was a regular topic of conversation. In the midst of these diatribes, many analysts began to speculate which large and financially sound firms would find the opportunity to acquire smaller competitors at distressed prices. (In BreitBurn's case, the common share price dipped as low as $4.55 per share.)

A merger or acquisition does not eliminate a share class. Barring assignment through receivership in a bankruptcy proceeding, merger or acquisition transactions simply transfer corporate obligations to the new or acquiring entity. Put simply, were a firm to step in and purchase BreitBurn (or any other corporation) in distressed circumstances, the purchasing firm acquires all of BreitBurn's obligations – including the obligations of the preferred share class. In this specific case, there is a change of control clause which provides that the entity will have the option to redeem the shares plus any unpaid dividends within 120 days at par value. If they do not exercise this right, then the shareholder, under certain circumstances, will have the option to convert their shares into common shares of the new entity. Without needlessly going into a thorough review of what those options are, please accept that the purpose of highlighting this scenario is that acquisition or merger of the corporation, even if in distress, does not obliterate the preferred shareholder or their respective value in the entity.

ABOUT THE AUTHOR

Michael F. Greco, CFP®, ChFC graduated from Lafayette College with a joint degree in Mathematics & Economics. His first foray into the financial industry was in the Treasury Department of M&T Bank, where Michael worked on the fixed-income desk. There he traded Fed Funds, Treasuries, Foreign Currency and assisted in the analysis of CMOs and Mortgage-backed securities.

In 1996, Michael transitioned to the retail side of financial services as a registered representative for a national wirehouse. Over the ensuring 20 years, Michael earned the Certified Financial Planner® designation and the Chartered Financial Consultant designation through the American College, eventually becoming the cofounder and managing partner of GCI Financial Group, Inc. where he serves as Chief Investment Officer and Director of Financial Planning. He is charged with overseeing the firm's discretionary wealth management activities.

Michael has written featured articles for a number of industry trade publications. He has been interviewed for various media forums, including National Public Radio and financial journals such as *Fortune*. He has been an adjunct professor of Economics & Banking at Seton Hall University. He also serves as an industry panelist arbitrator in the Financial Industry Regulatory Authority (FINRA) Dispute Resolution Forum.

He resides in New Jersey with his wife and three children.

Made in United States
Troutdale, OR
07/29/2023

11670860R00031